NEWSLETTERS AND PRESS RELEASES

BULLET GUIDE

Hodder Education, 338 Euston Road, London NW1 3BH

Hodder Education is an Hachette UK company

First published in UK 2012 by Hodder Education

This edition published 2012

www.hoddereducation.co.uk

Typeset by Stephen Rowling/Springworks

Printed in Spain

NEWSLETTERS AND PRESS RELEASES

BULLET GUIDE

Brian Salter

About the author

Brian Salter began his career at the BBC, where he produced and presented features and business and current affairs programmes. He left the BBC to join Heathrow Airport as Media Relations Manager immediately following the bombing of Pan Am Flight 103 over Lockerbie, and was responsible for improving relations with the resident press and for crisis communications at the airport. From there, he moved to a variety of roles in communications, and by the 1990s he had started his own consultancy, advising companies and giving training on public relations, marketing and presentation techniques, as well as Internet technology for business use when it was still in its infancy. In 1999 he moved to the Middle East, working in Saudi Arabia, Abu Dhabi and Dubai, and thence to China where he is currently working as a journalist in Beijing.

Contents

Introduction

At first glance, most **press releases** look simple and harmless enough – but even the biggest companies agonize over them.

It's an unfortunate fact that many press releases the world over are pretty dreadful. It is said that fully **99%** of all press releases get thrown straight in the bin by magazine and newspaper editors who are weary of being sent such rubbish – many of them written by PR agencies who are charging their clients a hefty fee!

The bottom line is that, to make the stories we tell **newsworthy**, we have to strive to hit the right buttons with the media, thereby increasing the chances of seeing those stories in the press.

And nowadays, of course, there is a much bigger choice of outlets for our stories than ever before, with countless online opportunities undreamt of only a few years ago.

But **why** are we thinking of issuing a press release in the first place? The answer might sound obvious – but very often people issue releases without a clear goal in mind – sometimes simply because the boss has told them to do so!

The way you **structure** a press release is also important, and can make or break its success in being picked up and used.

Company **newsletters** and **magazines**, too, can be highly flexible marketing tools. Well written and produced, they deliver the right message to the right audience in the right way. Many are professionally produced, but, equally, many fail for a number of reasons, as often as not because the entire process has not been thought through properly.

In this book we will be looking at some of the **basic considerations** that need to be taken when planning to publicize a company's products or services and at how to avoid many of the **common pitfalls** in order to inform and educate shareholders, reassure and persuade customers, recognize and motivate staff, and attract new business.

1 Promoting your business

Press releases and newsletters are two of the most effective ways of getting your point of view out to your target audiences

Promoting a business is an ongoing challenge for all companies, and **getting the right publicity** for a local campaign can **make or break its outcome**.

No matter if you …

* have a **new product** to launch
* are organizing a **demonstration**
* want to **publicize** your hobby group
* are **launching a campaign**

… you will have a **much better chance of success** if you tell people using newsletters and press releases.

A press release is the standard way of communicating with **journalists** – and journalists are your **conduit** to reaching your **target audiences** through the **media**:

* TV
* radio
* printed media

… and – to a lesser degree –

* through the World Wide Web.

If **written well**, a press release will tell them what the story is all about at a glance – giving all the essential information they need to make your story pertinent to their viewers, listeners and readers.

Journalists get inundated with press releases every day, so, if you want your voice to be heard, read on to make sure that yours **stands out from the crowd**.

Press releases

Writing a press release is one of the best ways to generate some **free publicity**.

But with the (relatively) recent rise of the Internet, the media landscape is changing, and with **social media** 'ordinary' people without any training are fast becoming the ones creating media.

So journalists are getting squeezed to produce more from – often – fewer resources, and anything you can do to help them fill their air time or column inches will end up in a **win–win situation** – for them and for you.

4

Imagine the scenario: you're a journalist with over 50 press releases sitting in your email inbox.

The first one you read is:

1 four pages long
2 has typing errors and grammatical mistakes
3 rambles on.

The second is:

1 short
2 easy to read
3 sticks to the point.

Which one would you prefer?

Journalists take about **ten seconds** to decide whether or not to use a release; and, amazingly, **two-thirds** of those releases head straight for the rubbish bin, many of them written by so-called professionals.

Newsletters

Whereas press releases are targeted at journalists, newsletters can be a useful conduit directly to your target audiences.

Sending newsletters to customers and prospects is a **highly effective marketing strategy**. They can be used:

* as **direct mail** to your prospects and customers
* in your **information** and **media kits**
* by your **salespeople** for handing out when making sales calls
* at **trade shows**
* for **prospects** and **customers** who come into your place of business
* to capture **names of prospects** who visit your website.

Newsletters delivered electronically (known as **ezines**) have also gained rapid acceptance for the same reasons that email is now often preferred over printed correspondence.

Newsletters are incredibly **inexpensive** to produce and distribute over the Internet, and this has led to around **half a million** newsletter titles being published on the web and via email **every month**.

They are a great way to **remind** people about your website, while also offering a chance to **develop trust** between your visitors and yourself. Marketers know only too well that, on the faceless Internet, **trust is everything**!

Cost-effective and informative

The ultra low cost of producing an electronic newsletter has meant that **any group** with an obscure or minority interest can now **viably publish** its own newsletter.

Hence, most Internet newsletters have a distribution of fewer than a thousand, and many have memberships in the low hundreds or even fewer.

But the cost of producing printed newsletters has also fallen dramatically in recent years, meaning that they, too, are a viable means of reaching your target audience.

Many businesses churn out **hard sell materials**, such as

✳ leaflets
✳ brochures

which concentrate on getting out their advertising messages.

This is all very well … but writing a business newsletter is a **softer**, more **opinion-forming** approach.

A good business newsletter is filled with **useful pieces of information** that allow the readers to browse through the sections that interest them in just two or three minutes.

A business newsletter should aim to educate and inform – but rarely should it be used for an outright sale.

TOP TIP
The idea is simple: to create a good climate of opinion among your end readers.

Communication is the key

It is said that, in today's Internet age, success is dependent not on whom you know, but on **how much you know.**

People hate being sold to. Rather, they want information about their industry and about new products and services.

A number of studies have shown that one of the main reasons that customers stop buying from a company is because of a lack of communication on the part of the business. Communication is the key to building relationships and keeping customers satisfied.

Engaging your prospects and customers with a newsletter will not only lead to **more sales**, but **more referrals** as well.

10

Of all the marketing options available to a business, the humble newsletter has stood the test of time.

Nowadays there are so many channels through which you can deliver a newsletter:

* by email
* over the Internet
* offline in print and through the post.

Newsletters come in all different shapes and sizes, but the one **over-riding principle** is exactly the same – they **remind** customers and prospective customers that your **product** or **service** exists.

Those written to help promote your business can be among the most effective … And that is something which is likely to be as true tomorrow as it is today.

2 Key messaging

Before beginning to write any press release or newsletter it is critically important to know what it is you want to say and to maintain consistency of your message to enable credibility

. . . .

Consistency with previous communications creates a **strong impression** and helps people remember your **core messages**.

Although a given message may be 'tweaked' or 'massaged' for different audiences, the **core messages** should not vary. Read on to find out how to make the most of your key messages.

Any news you add to a press release or newsletter should be augmented by your key messages.

This helps to reinforce the brand image and shapes the perception of your organization or product, which is one of the main reasons for sending out a release or newsletter in the first place.

So you must

* understand the public's interest in your business
* understand the press and their needs

… in order to deal effectively with the 'perception' of the company, product or yourself.

Remember who your real audience is, and what you want them to know!

Who is your audience?

In developing your key messages you must ensure that you:

* **Craft messages** for specific audiences.
* Talk in terms that your audience will **understand and care about**.
* **Simplify statements** — eliminating jargon and acronyms where possible.
* Determine which issues are **important to your audience**.
* Decide which issues are **negative/positive**.
* Develop **positive responses** for negative issues.

At all times you should remember the so-called WISH list …

* **W**ho are you talking to; what do you want them to think, do and feel; and what's in it for them?
* **I**s your message credible?
* **S**hape it into a quotable soundbite – avoid corporate jargon.
* **H**ave you got facts, examples and anecdotes to support it?

And you should always support your messages with:

* examples
* anecdotes
* analogies
* third-party endorsements
* personal experiences
* facts
* statistics
* the findings of research.

What do you want to say?

So, when writing your press release or story in a newsletter, you need to:

* **Tell your story** with the headline first.
* **Follow up** with your key messages.
* Add **supporting details.**
* Bring up other **secondary messages** if time/space allows.

Key messages form the foundation of a PR or communications plan. They can reinforce what audiences believe about you and your projects, or they can counter your audience's current beliefs and work to change its opinions.

TOP TIP
A key message is essentially what you want your audience to 'take away' from the story and recall when thinking about your product or brand.

Key messages are sometimes known as **BBQ statements** – what you want your target audience to say when they are discussing the topic around a barbecue or in a doctor's waiting room.

The marketplace is so thick with information competing for people's attention that you need to find some way of hacking through it.

Key messages help focus on **what's really important,** both to you and to your audience. They get **right to the point**, delivering critical information without wasting the audience's time with **unnecessary details**.

The owners, executives, company spokespersons, ALL employees, suppliers, and partners – anyone with a stake in the success of the business or industry – should **understand and use these messages**.

Reflect your audience

Your news release or newsletter will need to work hand in hand with a PR campaign to introduce new information, relating any messages to what the receiver already knows.

This is achieved by:

* repetition
* creating an environment in which messages are most likely to be heard
* keeping it interesting.

So we need to:

1 support with evidence
2 reflect stakeholders' understanding
3 be distinctive
4 be credible
5 drive our agenda
6 avoid negativity
7 enhance positivity
8 use our brand(s).

When you start to develop the message the first thing to consider is why you are creating this message and what you want to achieve with it:

* Start from scratch, listing key points about the topic.
* Write as many as you can think of, and then mix and match, combine and condense, cut and paste ruthlessly until you've got three or four brief bullet points that deliver the information your audience really needs to know.

Think like your audience – get inside their heads – so that you can focus on the key points they want and need to know.

A message will not be believed if it is contrary to the predispositions of the receiver

The anatomy of a key message

The anatomy of a key message can be expressed as:

claim = fact + example

A **claim** is what you want stakeholders to believe.

For example: 'Our company is the most innovative developer in the field.'

A **fact** is indisputable proof that what you claim is true.

For example: 'Our company won the Most Innovative Developer Award in 2011.'

Many communication efforts fail because they target everyone.

In reality, most outreach strategies should **target** a **specific group** of people.

Summary

1 Have **one main message** with up to three underlying themes to support it.
2 All messages should **support** the organization's main goals.
3 Messages shouldn't change frequently. To have **impact** they have to be **repeated** over and over again.
4 Messages can be **tailored** for specific audiences, while still remaining **constant**.
5 **Consistent messages** should pass through all of your communication efforts, not just when you write a press release or newsletter.
6 Messages must be **simple**. They are ideas that can be explained in a sentence or two – if they require a paragraph or two, keep working.
7 Messages take time to create – **don't rush** the process.

3 Structuring a press release

The way that you structure a release is so important that it should be at the very top of every aspiring PR practitioner's training list

The first thing that journalists see is the headline – if that doesn't **grab their attention**, your press release is heading for the dustbin.

The reason newspapers use **bold, attention-grabbing headlines** is because they work.

You can deploy the same strategy **to grab the attention** of the journalists you are trying to reach.

Read on to find out how to structure your press release for maximum impact.

The headline is the most important part of your press release

You should aim to use the so-called **'inverted pyramid'**, with the most important information at the top, the next most important information in the second paragraph, and so on.

The idea is that, if someone stops reading after the first or the second or the third paragraph, they will still know what the entire story is about, albeit the person who reads further down will have more detail on the story being told.

So it is important to tell the entire story in the headline and, if necessary, a subhead.

Comprehensive and concise

If your story is worth telling, you should ensure that you do **everything possible** to offer up the information reporters want.

So you should always give a **contact name** with phone number(s) and an email address somewhere prominent (I usually add these in a *Notes for Editors* section at the end).

Remember to **date** the release and indicate when, ideally, you want the information released, for example in time for a product launch.

You should refrain from **verbosity** and try to keep the release to one or two pages whenever possible.

If there is really so much background information you *have* to tell the journalist, it is best to put this in the *Notes for Editors* section.

One of the most common faults in news release writing is the use of sloppy language and verbosity.

So you should:

1 **Cut excess fat**, mentally eliminating words and phrases.
2 Keep your focus tight, concentrating on the **story in hand.**
3 **Cut back** on adjectives and adverbs and use strong nouns and verbs.

> **TOP TIP**
> Adding descriptive words slows the pace of reading and buries your message. Don't make readers search the text to find the substance.

The journalists' test

All press releases should answer journalists' six basic questions:

1 Who?
2 What?
3 Where?

4 When?
5 Why?
6 How?

This means that you must put yourself in the place of the journalist reading your release and test whether all these questions have been answered.

If you were an assignment editor with a desk piled high with press releases, would you go for one that is:

* three pages long and written in a florid style?

Or one that is:

* short, to the point, easy to read, and answers those six questions?

If you keep this test at the back of your mind, you really can't go wrong!

● Remember the journalists' test … make their life easy and they are more likely to use your press release

A picture paints a thousand words

Photos and graphics can be a powerful publicity tool – but only if you use them well.

A **good photo** can move your article from the back of a magazine to the front, and supplying a **feature picture** instead of a simple headshot helps bring your story to life.

The vast majority of publications now prefer **digital pictures**, provided that the quality is sufficiently good:

* Newspapers typically need a resolution not less than **200 dpi** (generated by a 3 or 4 megapixel camera).
* Magazines require much better – **300 dpi** (from a 6 megapixel camera) being the minimum acceptable quality.

When submitting releases:

1 Ensure that there are good-quality photos of all experts who might be interviewed by the media.

2 Consider asking the photographer to shoot experts *in situ*. A construction executive might be holding a hard hat for instance.

3 Have interior and exterior shots of the company available in case requested by the media.

4 Submit photos with news releases about routine announcements such as new hires, promotions, retirements, awards, etc.

5 Pie charts, bar charts and other **graphics** can help readers understand complicated issues such as budgets. Offer to supply raw information to media outlets so that they can create their own.

6 If sponsoring an event, call the **photo desk** at the local newspaper and let photographers know what's happening.

7 Make sure that all photos are scanned at **print-quality 300 dpi** and available for instant download at your website, preferably under a button called 'Media Resources'.

8 Never, ever ask the media to take photos of a cheque-passing, ground-breaking or ribbon-cutting ceremony. They hate non-news stories such as these! Be creative and offer something more interesting!

Spreading the news

Many businesses send out a brief press release and headshot when **someone new** is hired or a **major promotion** is made.

But, be sure to explain why the move is **significant** to the company – and perhaps the market – as a whole. It may be enough to lift the story from a back page to one of the news pages.

And a sharp business editor will see that your company is doing something far more significant than just taking on new staff.

A **media alert** is essentially a memo from you to media assignment editors, city desk editors and others, who then decide whether a particular news event is **worth covering**.

It's used to alert the press about:

* news conferences
* charity events
* publicity 'stunts'
* other events.

In just a few seconds, you should tell the journalist:

* about the event
* how to cover it
* why it's important that the media outlet covers it.

Most media alerts fail on the third point and so this is where you need to exert most effort.

4 Writing a press release

The headline is the first thing – and sometimes the only thing – an editor will read

Headlines must be compelling. On average:

* 8 out of 10 journalists will read headline copy.
* Only 2 out of 10 will read the rest.

So create headlines with impact – read on to find out how.

Never use the **past tense** as this will make your announcement sound like **old news**.

The most effective words in a news release headline are eye-catching words such as:

* 'announces'   * 'new'.

Comparative words such as:

* 'better'
* 'more'

can also draw attention to your article.

A **dateline** should precede the start of the text to tell the journalist where and when it is being released.

It is usually written in bold or capitalized, for example 'Leeds, 29 June 2011'.

Although it used to be common practice to use embargoes, in effect requesting a journalist to hold back the story until a specific time, the growth of the Internet and online reporting makes this a dangerous practice.

The beginning

The **first paragraph** of your release should encapsulate all the main facts and include the name of your company and the product/service/event you are announcing.

The **first sentence** should be direct, relate what is going on, and convey the level of importance of the news.

This introductory paragraph, along with the headline, is often all an editor will have time to read.

Many releases are rejected due to a failure to include any news in the first paragraph.

A **quote**, or recorded statement from an officer of the company, should – where possible – be included within the text.

It can **personalize the release** and, although most journalists will seek their own quotes by following up releases with interviews, journalists on a tight deadline may well use the quote to imply that they have done more research on the story that they actually did!

Avoid pointless platitudes such as:

✳ 'we are delighted …'

or

✳ 'we are proud to announce …'.

These add nothing to the story.

Try to introduce a **pertinent element** that hasn't been mentioned elsewhere in the release.

The middle

Relate the most newsworthy aspects first.

Subsequent paragraphs should provide supporting information in a descending hierarchy of importance.

Acronyms and abbreviations should be avoided. If used, spell them out in the first instance – for example, electronic point of sale (EPOS) – and then use them in the abbreviated form thereafter.

> **TOP TIP**
> Never use claims such as 'the world's no. 1 widget', or 'our widget is totally unique' (unless you can back it up with published research!) and avoid puffery such as 'our magnificent new service'.

The end

You should mark the end of your news release by putting '–end–' on a new line, after the last line of copy, so that editors know that there is no further news.

And then make sure to include in your *Notes to Editors* section a **'boilerplate'** which gives background information on your company:

* when it was launched
* where it is headquartered
* any particular achievements
* main areas of activity
* any additional information not provided in the body of the release.

Boilerplates can be revised periodically, but they should maintain consistency.

Contact details go at the bottom.

Journalists' tips

A press release should always be sent out on a company letterhead, with contact information listed at the top and bottom

If a company letterhead is not available, a **company logo** should be added so that the document is clearly an official communication.

You should use **clean fonts** such as Times New Roman or **Arial**, which are universally found on computers. If you use a special font, this will be replaced with a standard font on the recipients' machines, thereby losing your layout.

In the 'old days' (i.e. pre-PC) it was normal to double space each line, but nowadays this is no longer necessary.

Before any release is sent out to the world at large, it should always be **checked** for spelling and grammatical errors.

Nothing is guaranteed to make a worse impression with the recipient than a release with errors in it.

TOP TIP

Most newspapers and magazines insist that a 'second pair of eyes' is used to check over each story before publication, as it is all too easy for the original writer to 'see' what he or she expects to see, rather than what is actually there! Press release writers should follow the same example.

Summary

In summary, by following these simple tips you can elevate the chances of your press release being picked up and used by the media. Ensure that every release you send out contains the following:

1 **contact details** shown prominently
2 a **date**, ideally the same as the day on which it is sent
3 a **snappy headline**, which is interesting, makes sense and grabs attention
4 an introductory paragraph with a quick overall **summary** of the story, which is rock solid, to the point and interesting
5 a **web link** from the company name, so that the journalist can click through for more information
6 **a quote** showing the title of the person being quoted and their full name – the more interesting the quote, the greater the chance it will be used
7 the **price** of a new product or service and information on **availability**, along with any launch offers, etc.

Bullet Guide: Newsletters and Press Releases

8 **pictures**, which can determine whether a story gets used or not, especially if there is a good visual angle
9 information on whether senior personnel are available for **interview**
10 **Notes for Editors** for anything else you can think of, such as a company's unique selling points.

5 Essential reading

It's an unfortunate fact that many press releases the world over are pretty dreadful

· ·

XYZ Company, a leading supplier of software, announced today the availability of its latest product, the XYZ 4.2 v3, which will revolutionize the microtechnology industry.
'This will revolutionize the microtechnology industry,' said Nigel Glover, XYZ's CEO.

Why do they do it?

Instead of conforming to the conventional approach – which is dated, formulaic and dull – choose a **better model** to follow. Read on to find out how.

Try these alternatives:

* Write a feature lead.
* Lead with the benefits.
* Try a tipsheet suggesting ways in which your product could be used.

A feature story press release resembles a magazine article, and is written in a more entertaining manner. The feature often sets the tone and background before introducing the main topic.

Include enough information to allow a busy editor to use the story without calling you, and write the story in pyramid news style – with less essential information towards the end.

Tell a good story

Some company bosses believe that, as their product is used by so many people, they should have coverage in every major newspaper and on every broadcast network.

But being prevalent doesn't mean that the story is interesting or timely … or even that there is a story at all!

Brainstorm with colleagues what could make your item newsworthy:

1 Put a spin on something ordinary.
2 Identify something unusual that makes your product unique.

And you have a good chance of turning a dull story into something usable.

For instance, if you were promoting a toothbrush:

* Create a controversy: for example, claim that 90% of people use their toothbrush for far too long.
* Offer surprising facts about your product: for example, how long ago people were using toothbrushes surprisingly similar to today's.
* Piggyback on the news: for example, play up the connection if there's a toothbrush scene in a new feature film.

Or, promoting a mobile phone:

* Give an award: for example, a prize for the most unusual telephone call.
* Show an unexpected group of people using your product, for example, toddlers.
* Do a survey: for example, what percentage of people never leave the house without their mobile phone.

Creative ideas

* Compile a set of useful tips: for example, ten things you should not do with a toothbrush.
* Publicize a worthy cause: for example, donate your product to a good cause.
* Offer a freebie: for example, free phones for disabled school kids.
* Find a new use for your product: for example, use a toothbrush to clean jewellery.
* Tie in with economic trends: for example, what toothbrush sales reveal about the latest recession.

* Sponsor a charity event: for example, hold a Toothbrush Ball.
* Do something environmental: for example, recyclable mobile phones.
* Celebrate an anniversary: for example, your ten millionth toothbrush sold.
* Create product variations: for example, a left-handed toothbrush.
* Get offbeat endorsements: from a racing driver, for example.
* Run an event for kids: for example, develop a dental road show that travels to schools explaining about tooth decay.

Lists

You could even start a **Hall of Fame**.

All you have to do is find some of your industry's top movers and shakers and, once a year, induct them into your Hall of Fame.

You then send out a press release explaining what is special about these particular people.

And each year you induct some more members and send out yet another release.

> **TOP TIP**
> The press love things like this as they are **light hearted** and easily **fill column inches**.

There are plenty of other types of list you can send out:

* the best
* the worst
* the most

* the least
* the top ten
* the bottom ten

… and so on.

The majority of tabloid newspapers thrive on **lists** as they present the editor with easy to use, light-hearted trivia, which many people love to read.

Some of the most successful lists include **controversial areas** such as:

* the worst dressed man
* the most boring actor
* the politician with the worst taste

… and so on.

TOP TIP
The more controversial the list, the better the chance it has of being used, as long as it doesn't cross that fine line into libel.

Other angles

If you can add a **local angle** to an international news story, you might be able to 'piggyback' on the coverage by providing a different angle to the news outlets, which, in the main, want to differentiate themselves from the competition.

Better still, if you can find a way to **highlight the unusual**, you might be able to make your story go viral – perhaps with an accompanying video uploaded to YouTube.

You can search for ideas simply by entering your industry field into something like Google News and seeing what bizarre stories are available. **Then take one of the ideas and develop it further.**

But remember, **you are fooling nobody**, so don't pretend to the journalists that your lists or unusual angles are earth-shatteringly important.

Both sides can 'play the game' in a win–win situation.

In general, you should try to avoid **criticizing** or **embarrassing** anyone.

And you should always keep it **relevant** to your industry or profession.

A good publicist can quite literally invent a story that the news media will eat up.

Most businesses overlook many opportunities to send out a press release and get some media coverage. They are too busy thinking about how the story is about them, rather than how they can **fit into the story**.

6 Distributing press releases

Many would argue that the distribution of a news release is more taxing than the writing itself

The world is rapidly shrinking, and the media are now a global industry.

Distribution of a story is much more than sending out a release to a handful of editors.

To be effective, distribution needs to target:

* wire services (news agencies)
* bloggers
* social networking communities
* online news services
* and more

… **in addition** to newspapers and magazines. Read on to discover how to make distribution most effective with the least hassle.

But before sending anything out to anyone, you need to check, check and **check again.**

Bigger businesses often have a series of executives who will want to **review** the release copy before it goes to the press.

For small businesses, it is a good idea to have someone else **proofread** the copy as it is all too easy to miss a mistake you have made – be it factual, grammatical or spelling.

This is why most publications demand that all copy should be **checked** by someone who did not write the item.

Compiling contacts

If you've written the release and are now considering whom to send it to, you've actually gone about it the wrong way!

This is because the release needs to be matched as far as possible to the needs and predispositions of the media outlets to which it will be sent.

Media outlets can have a high turnover rate, so an updated media contact list is essential.

One of the easiest ways of finding up-to-date contacts is to get on to the Internet and do a search of:

1 local media
2 national media
3 trade media
4 other specialist media.

It's always a good idea, too, to make up **your own media contact list** from your researches – though it has to be kept up to date to make it usable at all.

While you're contacting conventional media outlets, don't forget to send your information to other outlets that accept this type of news:

* Internet newsgroups
* electronic newsletters
* web-based mailing lists.

Bloggers, too, are often happy to receive news pitched via their website.

There are also directories of media outlets – both printed and updated electronic versions – which takes a lot of the guesswork out of where to send your release, though these can be expensive to purchase or subscribe to.

Targeting contacts

Each release should be **targeted at specific media outlets** and sent to reporters who cover that sector. (You can usually find specific names from the outlet's website.)

For example, if your business operates in the UK's civil engineering sector, you would target:

1 the UK's civil engineering publications
2 journalists writing for national newspapers and magazines
3 freelancers who cover this topic
4 Internet sites that specialize in civil engineering matters.

But if you are launching a service aimed solely at the residents of Litchfield, you would target only the **local press** in that area.

TOP TIP
If you are targeting different press sectors, write multiple releases rather than one 'catch-all' release.

Getting your story out is only half the battle. Making sure it's seen is the other half!

Although you may well be sending out a picture with your release to the printed media, consider sending more images and video clips with your press release when targeting **online media.**

But remember to send only links to these. **DO NOT** send out large files to any media outlet, otherwise you will find yourself blocked in the future, and it is unlikely that your story will be used at all.

For greater coverage, set up a press room on your company website so that reporters can access your entire library of releases in the future.

Distribution tips

Send your release by email, and place the release in the **body of the email** itself. If you must use an attachment, make sure it is in plain text or is an RTF (rich text format) file.

Microsoft Word documents are universally acceptable, but remember that not everyone can read the newer '.docx' format yet, so send only '.doc' format files.

As a general rule, it is best not to send **PDF files**, unless there are a number of graphics (e.g. charts and diagrams) contained in the body of the release. Make sure that the contents of the PDF file can be copied and pasted.

TOP TIP
Use your headline as the subject line of the email to make it easily identifiable.

If you don't feel up to the task of distributing your news release yourself, there are plenty of commercial services that will do this for a fee.

If you have a major announcement to make that absolutely must get into the general media, you might find this cost-effective, especially if you wish to target foreign publications.

You will find many such agencies listed on the Internet, such as:

* Cision
* Daryl Willcox Publishing
* Freepressreleases.co.uk
* PR Newswire
* PRWeb
* Pressbox
* Press Dispensary
* PressWire
* Vocus.

Generally their fees range between around £50 and £250 per release.

Following up

It is sometimes useful to follow up your press release with a call to the journalists to see if your company news is of interest to them.

But never call a journalist to ask if he or she received your release! Be more subtle, asking instead if there is a particular angle about your story that would be of further help.

But bear in mind that journalists hate being pestered by people sending out releases. If they are interested, they'll contact you for further information or to request a company logo or photo – not the other way around!

If journalists do get in touch, always provide timely and accurate information, remembering that they will be working to a deadline.

70

It is a good idea to **track** whether your announcement appears anywhere in the press. Obviously if a journalist comes back to you for further information, that is always a good place to search first.

Otherwise a good place to look is on one of the Internet search engines that specialize in monitoring news outlets – such as:

* www.bing.com/news
* daylife.com
* news.google.com
* www.magportal.com
* www.newslookup.com
* www.pandia.com
* www.topix.com
* news.yahoo.com

Many of these sites will enable you to set up 'alerts', so that you don't need to keep checking back.

Alternatively you might wish to engage a **professional monitoring service**, of which there are several.

7 Writing newsletters

One of the best ways of communicating news and information to prospects and customers is by newsletter

* It helps companies maintain a **relationship** with customers, and cultivate **prospects** who aren't yet ready to buy.
* **It positions you as an industry expert**, and, if done well, can lead to more referrals, and more sales.

Newsletters are far more **cost-effective** than advertising material, and they are easy to create.

Newsletters come in all shapes and sizes, but their principal role is to remind customers and prospects that your product or service exists.

Read on to find out how to write a winning newsletter.

Most businesses tend to concentrate on hard-sell advertising materials to sell their products and services.

But newsletters give you the opportunity to let your prospects and customers know your opinions on a wide variety of topics.

There are few marketing methods that can deliver the same level of customer loyalty and impact as a newsletter.

But before you produce the newsletter, you need to determine its **purpose**.

∗ Who are you writing it for?

Obviously you need to **cater specifically** for this group of people.

How often?

A few years back, when printing was the preferred method of publishing a newsletter, production costs were relatively high – but the Internet and email have changed all that.

Nowadays newsletters are cheap to produce and distribute.

Whether you choose to publish:

* online
* in print

… newsletters work only when distributed on a **regular** and **consistent** basis.

If you are publishing offline, your newsletter needs to be mailed monthly or bi-monthly, but no fewer than **six times a year.**

If you are publishing online, the norm is to publish weekly or bi-weekly, but not less than **once a month.**

What to include?

People today don't want to be sold to. Instead they want relevant information that can help them make up their own minds about new products and services.

Studies consistently show that prospects respond better to **relevant content** than to a heavy duty sales pitch.

So for your newsletter content you should aim to provide at the minimum:

* information about your business in order to lend credibility
* information about your people to improve the connection between reader and company employees
* statistics about your business, including customer satisfaction ratings
* a 'frequently asked questions' section, which identifies at least five of the queries you most commonly receive.

The basics

Most successful newsletters concentrate on getting the basics absolutely correct.

1 **Content** With so many newsletter titles on the web, **great content matters**, perhaps more so than ever before.
2 **Style** Your newsletter needs to reflect an easily identifiable style and stick to it. Is it light hearted or serious? Worthy or fun? Your readers need to know **what to expect** when they receive your newsletter.
3 **Frequency** Rigidly stick to your publishing schedule so that people know **when to expect** delivery.
4 **Credibility** If your readers do not believe the content, then the newsletter will surely fail.
5 **Integrity** Avoid turning the newsletter into one long relentless sales pitch. **It fools nobody.**

Content

One of the greatest challenges for any newsletter editor is finding or producing the content.

But many newsletter editors act the part of:

* editor
* subeditor
* designer
* publisher
* the ONLY contributor

… all rolled into one!

To get help with producing content, you should ask your own people to contribute an article. Give them a **deadline** and a **word count** as this acts as an incentive for them to deliver something on time.

And to keep up the pressure, send a **gentle reminder** two or three days before their deadline to ensure that you get that necessary content!

Interviews

If your people are too busy to write you an article, record someone chatting to you.

Remember to ask them **open-ended questions**, such as:

* Who?
* What?
* Why?

* When?
* Where?
* How?

… or you might simply get a series of yes and no answers, which will not help you in the slightest.

Then transcribe the conversation and edit it down into an article.

Remember to keep the interview rich in **problem solving** and **benefits** as that is what most people want to read about.

Other features

Also of interest is:

* news of industry trends
* buying patterns
* inventory levels
* employment
* products
* regulation.

The more industry focused, the better.

Case studies spelling out how real companies solved real-world problems are also well received by readers.

Try to use a **mix** of 'how to' articles and items designed to get people to change their perspectives.

Above all, your newsletter should be a **pleasure to read**, rather than a worthy plod through your industry.

Try adding one of the following:

* a cartoon
* some trivia
* a quote of the day
* something else amusing.

Visual impact

The front page needs to be well designed, appealing, and hard hitting to entice people to read on.

Graphics always add to the appeal of a newsletter. You should include:

* charts
* cartoons
* illustrations
* sidebars.

The 80/20 rule

Use your business newsletter writing to both **educate** and **inform** your reader. But only rarely use it to sell outright!

Follow the 80/20 rule:

* Use 80% of the space to talk about anything but your business.
* Use 20% to focus on your products and services.

Remember to use your newsletter as a door opener!

Short of inspiration?

Some newsletters '**overkill**' on such a narrow subject range that they end up losing their audience.

You must have **good content** if you want to keep your readers enthralled.

There are numerous articles or 'fillers' that you could add to your newsletter. But, if you are short of inspiration, you can search the web for **syndicated content**.

Certain sites provide '**content streams**', whereby you can simply place a few lines of code on your web page, and forget about it.

The content provider either charges a fee for using their content, or benefits through increased traffic.

Free reprint articles are also widely available.

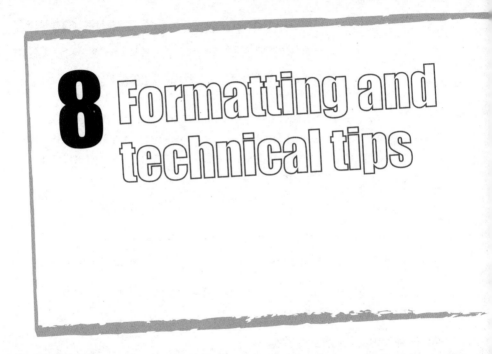

8 Formatting and technical tips

Whether you are publishing your newsletter in print or online, it should always reflect a consistent look and feel

There are a number of desktop publishing programs available that can be used for preparing your newsletter, ranging from the professional 'all-singing, all-dancing programs' such as:

* Adobe InDesign
* Quark Xpress

… to the very basic programs such as:

* Microsoft Publisher
* Serif PagePlus.

Many web page development programs, too, offer newsletter templates.

But don't even think about using Microsoft Word, which can be a nightmare for making small changes in layout! Read on to find out how to make the process painless.

One of the advantages of using dedicated page layout programs is that they allow the designer to **maintain consistency and make quick changes** to text throughout a document.

Style sheets are especially useful for laying out newsletters as they allow you to make changes that **affect the whole document**, rather than making them one paragraph at a time.

Not only does the use of styles save time, they help eliminate errors as changes are applied consistently throughout.

Styles

With **paragraph styles**, a designer can specify standard features such as:

* alignment
* indents
* space or rules above and below paragraphs
* hyphenation/widow and orphan control
* tabs
* colour.

Character styles such as:

* fonts, regular, bold and italic
* leading, kerning, tracking
* scaling
* colour

… cover some of the same features found in paragraph styles, but take priority so that you can make small changes to a paragraph without affecting the rest of that block.

Fonts

When choosing which fonts to use it is essential to consider the **end product**. Is the newsletter to be printed or electronic?

* If the former, you will need to ensure that you embed the fonts into the print-ready PDF file that you supply to the printer.
* If electronic, it is best to stick to **standard fonts** as your document will not display properly if end users do not have a copy of the particular fonts that you have used on their system (again, you could overcome this by embedding the fonts into a PDF version of your newsletter).

TOP TIP
If at all in doubt,
keep it simple!

Images

When it comes to deciding which **image resolution** to use, it again depends on whether it is a printed newsletter or an electronic one.

If **electronic**, you can set your image resolution to **72 dpi** (assuming that it is not expected to be printed off by the end user). A typical file size of 250 kB is quite adequate for images to illustrate features.

However, if the newsletter is to be **printed**, you will need to increase the resolution to **300 dpi.**

Typically, newsletters with print runs up to about 200 will be digitally printed, and larger print runs will be litho printed.

90

Colour images come in two formats:

* **RGB**   red, green, blue.
* **CMYK**   cyan, magenta, yellow, key (black).

For on-screen use, you will need to keep your images in RGB (because red + green + blue = white when projected).

But, for litho printing, red + green + blue would make black, so instead the printer uses CMYK images.

You can convert to/from RGB/CMYK using most image-processing programs such as Photoshop or PaintShop Pro.

Digital print machines can cope with either RGB or CMYK formats.

Layout

Always make sure that readers can see at a glance what can be found in your newsletter – and where.

So pay close attention to:

* the nameplate – the banner on the front with the name, logo, and issue number
* the table of contents
* contact information
* headlines
* subheads – to divide the articles into smaller sections
* page numbers
* bylines – the name and affiliation of the writer
* end signs – marking the end of an article
* photos/illustrations
* captions.

Have your newsletter content ready to go **before** you start to lay out the pages, rather than starting work before you have assembled the necessary articles.

And then, before attempting to lay out anything, put together a decent **template**.

Many programs come with **sample templates,** and you can also find many designs – both free and at a cost – on the Internet.

Obviously you will need different types of templates, depending on your final medium for distribution.

TOP TIP
Working from a ready-made newsletter template will speed up your work dramatically.

Distribution

Many people mistakenly think that it isn't worth starting up a newsletter unless they can command a huge audience.

Often the decision is made by the cost of distributing the newsletter. And that then impacts on whether to distribute:

1 **online** via email or the Internet
2 **offline** as a printed publication.

Initially, you will have to 'guestimate' how many copies to print off.

If you choose litho printing, it is best to **print more** than you need, as the run-on costs are normally insignificant compared with the set-up costs, which include making printing plates and performing test runs to get the colour balance correct.

If distributing over the Internet, consider offering an **RSS** (rich site summary or *really simple syndication*) feed, using news aggregator software, allowing your readers to access your content without having to visit your website.

You could also consider using a **hosted email service**, which allows you to offer both plain text and HTML versions of your newsletter.

It is often easier to let a professional third party handle subscribes, unsubscribes, bounces, white listing, CAN-SPAM compliance (to meet the requirements of US federal law when sending commercial email to customers) and list management. There are many agencies listed on the Internet.

Another online innovation is the use of 'autoresponders' to send out information at predetermined intervals.

Look up companies such as:

* www.aweber.com
* www.auto-responder.co.uk
* freeautobot.com.

9 Copyright

One of the **biggest problems** faced by editors that many ignore, or do not understand, is the subject of copyright.

Understanding copyright law is essential if you want to avoid costly lawsuits

Many break copyright law **unintentionally**, not even knowing that they have done anything illegal in the first place.

But ignorance is **no defence** in a court of law, and at the end of the day it is the editor who could be sued for a large sum of money.

Everyone who writes for, or edits, newsletters should be aware of the basic laws of copyright in order to avoid making a costly mistake! Read on to find out how to avoid this in your newsletter.

Please note that this chapter is based on UK copyright law – however, the situation in most of the rest of the world is very similar.

The **most common infringement** of copyright law occurs when an article from another source is reprinted in a different newsletter.

Many believe that, if they attribute the original source of the article, then they are allowed to reproduce anything that has already appeared in the public domain.

But this belief is a fallacy.

You can only reprint someone else's story if you first obtain **permission** – preferably in writing – both from the owners of the publication in which it first appeared and from the author (depending on who in fact owns the copyright).

What is protected?

You are allowed to write about the ideas contained in a copyrighted article, as **ideas** and **facts** cannot themselves be copyrighted.

It is only the **expression** of those ideas that is subject to copyright restriction.

So, for instance, if you read in a management book about a new training technique, this does not stop you explaining that technique in your publication, as long as you do not use the exact same words from the original book in your article.

This does not mean that you can copy the management training article and just change a few words here and there to make it appear somewhat different.

Copyright law also protects the **structure** and **'feel'** of the original article, so, if your words were different, but the overall flow and structure were the same, you would again be guilty of copyright infringement.

Often it is best to read the original article, then put it away and write your own article off the top of your head, summarizing the ideas in the original article that you found interesting, and at the same time adding your own take on the subject. In this case, obtaining the copyright holder's permission is not necessary.

TOP TIP
It is a good idea, for ethical reasons, to attribute the original information to the original author and publication.

What else is protected?

Copyright law covers a number of areas.

The most obvious is the one that stops others making copies (e.g. with a photocopier).

If your work can be performed in public, such as in a theatre, then that is also subject to copyright protection.

Displaying a work in public is another.

The right to modify it to suit a purpose not originally intended by the author – such as a screenplay based on your article – is another.

These reproduction rights normally expire **70 years** after their owner's death.

As well as ensuring that they do not transgress copyright laws, newsletter editors should also be interested in **protecting** their own information contained within their newsletters.

Protecting your original contents from unauthorized reproduction is surprisingly easy. Basically, you don't need to do anything!

The moment you have created your newsletter, **the law of copyright** applies to it without any need to register your work.

Assumptive rights

This protection is known as '**assumptive rights**'.

In general, it means that it is assumed that the person who wrote the publication or article has certain rights when it comes to how it can be used by others.

Some like to add the word '**Copyright**' to their work, or the internationally recognized symbol ©, together with a name and the date of its creation.

In most Western countries, however, it is not a **legal necessity** – owner's copyright is assumed regardless.

Nonetheless, it may act as a reminder to others that your work is copyrighted, and that, if anyone else wants to reproduce it, they do need to ask your **permission** first.

104

Open access

It may be that you would be only too delighted for others to reproduce your newsletter articles. In which case you need to term your work **'open access'**.

Open access grants anyone with an Internet connection the right to gain access to your entire published newsletter online at no cost whatsoever.

Although access is free, if the published work is protected by copyright, the end user may still be restricted in a number of ways.

So, for example, the user may use parts of your work to illustrate a lecture, with portions reproduced in a PowerPoint presentation.

But he or she would not be allowed to prepare a derivative work, such as another newsletter, if doing so could not be justified as 'fair use.'

All Rights Reserved

The term **All Rights Reserved** is also often used.

This implies that the owner would consider **relinquishing** or **transferring** one or more rights to the work, usually under a licence agreement or similar arrangement, in return for certain considerations.

Just because someone writes a piece of work does not necessarily mean that he or she owns the copyright.

For instance, if it was **commissioned** or created on someone else's behalf (such as a newsletter editor commissioning someone to write an article) then it's possible that it's the editor, not the author, who is the official copyright holder.

Protecting yourself

If you are responsible for a web-based newsletter, you could always have a copyright page spelling out what is and is not allowable.

For instance:

* The text contents and any photographs on this website are the property of XYZ Limited and its respective copyright holders.
* All logos, graphic designs and images are the express copyright of XYZ Limited.
* The content within this site may not be reproduced by any individual or entity, in whole or in part in any form whatsoever, without the prior express written consent of XYZ Limited.

10 Common mistakes

Although you may not necessarily want to attract the largest number of readers, it is self-defeating to give your potential audience a reason not to read your work in the first place

Despite the fact that the world is filled with newsletters of almost every description, there are a number of **themes** that run through the catalogue of mistakes most commonly made by newsletter editors – especially in their first publications.

Some of these mistakes are **easily avoided** and should be given high priority. After all, why turn off potential readers before they have even started? Read on to avoid these pitfalls.

No. 1 Not publishing regularly

If you announce that your newsletter will be published every month, then make sure that it is.

If you don't, your company will lose credibility and your readers will lose interest in your publication.

Often, newsletter editors are given this responsibility in addition to their normal everyday duties. But many people do not understand that to produce a quality product takes time and commitment.

TOP TIP
If you don't have the time or the people to devote to producing a newsletter, it might be better commissioning an external supplier to do it for you.

No. 2 Writing weak headlines

Your newsletter may have a plethora of interesting articles, but if they are given poor headlines, your readers are likely to skip over the story.

The headline can literally determine whether or not the article will be read.

One of the best ways of writing a catchy headline is to use a phrase or sentence that contains a **verb**.

Look for the most interesting points being made in the article and see if you can fashion a headline from them.

Remember The more descriptive a headline, the more likely it is to grab your interest!

No. 3 Writing weak lead sentences

The way you lead in to your article is also important. Just because a reader starts an article (having been tempted by your headline) does not mean that he or she will necessarily finish it.

Write an article with the **most important information** (as far as the reader is concerned) right at the beginning.

For instance, which would you find more interesting:

* 'The annual staff meeting was held at 3pm on 29 June in the reception area of the Simbacom HQ building …'
* 'Simbacom's CEO spoke about a new reward and incentive scheme, which he laid out in detail at the annual staff meeting …'

No. 4 Using too many type styles and fonts

To give your newsletter a feeling of uniformity, you should aim to use the same type style and size for the main text of all your articles. If your story is too long for the space available, don't reduce the type size in order to cram everything in, but carefully subedit the piece by cutting superfluous words and sentences.

Many successful publications use serif fonts such as Times New Roman, Georgia or Garamond for the body text, and a mixture of serif and sans-serif fonts (such as **Helvetica** or **Tahoma** or **Trebuchet**) for the headers.

No. 5 Using boring and predictable layouts

If all of your headlines are the same size, none will **stand out**.

Instead, generate greater interest in the more important stories by using larger headlines, and use smaller headlines for less important articles.

Similarly, vary the width of your articles, such that some spread across, say, three columns while others cover two or even one (for the smaller, less important stories).

This multi-width layout is far more visually pleasing than a layout in which all articles are of the same width.

No. 6 Not using pictures

In the majority of cases, the first thing that draws people's attention is the photo accompanying an article.

Using photos in a newsletter is probably the best way to **engage your readers** and make your newsletter look visually exciting.

Pictures also enhance the reader's experience by helping **cement** the gist of the story in the minds of your audience.

For instance, if you were writing about the appointment of a new marketing manager, the story is much more likely to be remembered if there is a photo of the new manager to accompany the article.

No. 7 Compromising people's privacy

With the high prevalence of spam on the Internet nowadays, most people are understandably **cautious** about having their email addresses broadcast to the world.

They may also be wary of **being identified** at all as recipients of your newsletter.

So when sending out your newsletter (or any promotional material, for that matter), desist from putting everyone's email address in the 'To' field so that all recipients can see everyone else's address as well.

Instead, put your own email address in the 'To' field and use the 'bcc' (blind carbon copy) field for everyone else.

No. 8 Bad hyperlinks

The use of **hyperlinks** in your online newsletter is a very useful way to share valuable information with your readers, be it background information to an article or more about your products and services and where to purchase them.

Many newsletters have incomplete or incorrect hyperlinks, which is **extremely frustrating** to readers who want to find out more.

Always **check your hyperlinks** and use full URL addresses (including the 'http://' at the beginning, as you may inadvertently have been successfully clicking a 'relative' URL on your machine, which is not valid on someone else's).

And finally ...

... while we are thinking about what *not* to do, here are a few ways to **promote** your newsletter:

* Send out one of your best issues as a **sample issue**, inviting people to sign up if they like it.
* Put a **sign-up form** on every page of your website.
* Offer a **free gift** for new subscribers.
* List your newsletter in **free ezine directories**, of which there are hundreds on the web.
* Plug your newsletter in your **email signature**.
* Advertise your newsletter on the back of your **business cards**.
* Become active in **online forums** where your readers hang out.